Motivating People

The Lessons Learned Series

Learn how the most accomplished leaders from around the globe have tackled their toughest challenges in the Harvard Business Press *Lessons Learned* series.

Concise and engaging, each volume in this series offers fourteen insightful essays by top leaders in industry, the public sector, and academia on the most pressing issues they've faced. The *Lessons Learned* series also offers all of the lessons in their original video format, free bonus videos, and other exclusive features on the 50 Lessons companion Web site **www.50lessons.com/people**.

Both in print and online, *Lessons Learned* contributors share surprisingly personal and insightful anecdotes and offer authoritative and practical advice drawn from their years of hard-won experience.

A crucial resource for today's busy executive, *Lessons Learned* gives you instant access to the wisdom and expertise of the world's most talented leaders.

Other books in the series:

Motivating People

LES50NS

www.50lessons.com/people

Boston, Massachusetts

Printed in the United States of America
13 12 11 10 09   5 4 3 2 1

Library of Congress Cataloging-in-Publication Data

Motivating people.
       p. cm. — (Lessons learned)
    ISBN 978-1-4221-3981-3 (pbk.)
 1.   Employee motivation. 2.   Leadership.
3.   Motivation (Psychology)
    HF5549.5.M63M663 2009
    658.3'14—dc22

                                        2009014939

A Note from the Publisher

executives, academics, and business thinkers speak directly and candidly about their triumphs and defeats. Taken together, these powerful stories offer the advice you'll need to take on tomorrow's challenges.

As you read this book, we encourage you to visit **www.50lessons.com/people** to view videos of these lessons as well as additional bonus material on this topic. You'll find not only new ways of looking at the world, but also the tried-and-true advice you need to illuminate the path forward.

⊰ CONTENTS ⊱

Contents

Motivating People

Praise and Support, Not Targets and Blame

Sir John Banham

Chairman, Johnson Matthey

THIS IS A lesson about how to instigate change in a hostile world. A long time ago, almost exactly twenty-five years ago, I was asked by Mrs. Thatcher and Michael

Heseltine to head up the Audit Commission. The Audit Commission is, and was then, there to ensure that local government—and now the National Health Service as well—secures economy, efficiency, and effectiveness in using resources. It has oversight of something like 10 to 15 percent of the entire gross national product. When I was asked to set it up, it had nothing: no bank account, no stationery, no staff, no board, and not even a title. Just nothing. It was three pages of legislation: the local government Finance Act of 1982, Section II. Serious competition for Mogadon—about the most boring stuff you can possibly imagine.

I had agreed that I would set up this institution with the objective of securing change in the way local government right across England and Wales was managed. And it's worked. Twenty-five years later, it is still going strong. I don't think they've put a foot wrong in all that time. And the way in which they secured that change was the exact reverse of what Mrs. Thatcher, probably

Praise and Support

Michael Heseltine, and certainly all the civil service expected. Instead of a command-and-control approach of targets—"You do it, we'll monitor it"—all the stuff that has still not worked in the National Health Service, what the Audit Commission did was find out who was doing things spectacularly well, photograph it, and celebrate it. And tell everyone else that if you can do it in Barnsley, you can do it anywhere.

In the case of local government, it's very easy because there are more than four hundred and eighty districts across the United Kingdom, and they are all doing the same things: collecting refuse, providing street lighting, in many cases operating schools, looking after elderly people, running police forces, and so on. I can absolutely assure you that in every aspect of the work of local government—or indeed the National Health Service—someone somewhere is doing it spectacularly. All you have to do is find out where, make sure it can be replicated and is not special to that particular place, then get out there and celebrate it.

Motivating People

That very simple, almost Dale Carnegie—
type insight into what motivates people,
which is praise and support, rather than
targets, blame, and auditing, has saved the
taxpayers billions of pounds a year.

I've never known people to get out of bed
in the morning for a key performance indi-
cator. People get out of bed in the morning
because they want to do a good job for their
clients or guests or whoever they are. At
Whitbread we employ sixty thousand people, and it's a terrific business because all
our colleagues and team members who look
after people know that their job is to look
after people. They don't have key performance indicators: we train them as well as we
possibly can, we empower them to get on
and do the job they'd like to be done.
They've all been guests themselves; they
know exactly how they would like to be
treated. And what we measure all the time
is guest satisfaction, how they think about
themselves in their job, as well as all the
other financial things that you would expect
us to look at.

Praise and Support

People are not driven by financial targets. They're driven by a wish to do a terrific job for whomever they see as their client. The job of management is to empower people to do that and to deliver that service and those benefits. The lesson of how to secure change in a hostile world is to remember that praise, reward, and empowerment are light-years more effective than blame, targets, monitoring, inspectorates, and all the assembly of the bureaucratic apparatus that has failed dismally to secure effective change throughout the public service for the last two decades.

TAKEAWAYS

- People are not driven by financial targets; they're driven by a wish to do a terrific job for whomever they see as their client.

Motivating People

⚓ The job of management is to empower people to do a terrific job.

⚓ Remember that praise, reward, and empowerment are light-years more effective than blame, targets, monitoring, inspectorates, and the assembly of the bureaucratic apparatus.

Unlocking Potential

Sir David Bell

Director for People, Pearson

WHEN I WORKED for the *Financial Times*, we decided to close our printing plant where a lot of people who had been with us a long time had given us an awful lot of problems. Nevertheless, we were faced with a situation where hundreds of them were going to lose their jobs. So, we decided to offer as many as wanted it the chance to retrain as

journalists. They didn't have a single quali-
fication among them. We developed a set
of structured questions and, in the end, we
took thirty of them through these questions
and offered eight of them training.

From this we learned that you're almost
always wrong when you assume that people
don't have ambition, can't do anything
more than they are already doing, and really
don't matter very much. We gave these guys a
six-month training program in London.
Ten years later, three of them are still working for us while the others became journalists elsewhere. These were people who'd
been separated from the floor I was on as a
journalist by six feet of concrete, but they
could have been on a different planet. We
were very proud of that.

We've now extended that philosophy in a
slightly different way; we've said to all thirty
thousand people in the business that we
want to talk to them about how they're doing
their present job and what they might do in
the future. Most of them say, "I'm quite
happy doing what I'm doing." Most people

are not particularly ambitious about doing other things; if they were it would be much harder to run a business. But many more than we think have ideas about what they would like to do. We are convinced that this process will give us lots of leads as to what people might do and whether they need more training to do it.

We've had people who say, "This is very dangerous. Just because you can play the piano doesn't mean you're going to end up as Chopin," or "Not everybody can be Tiger Woods because they can play golf." We have to structure this very carefully so we don't start with a program that raises expectations that we then can't meet. But we don't believe that's a reason for not doing it. On the contrary we believe that we have to structure this so we can understand what people would like to do and where we can give them a chance and unlock the talent that's there, which sometimes doesn't get noticed.

It doesn't matter what your qualifications are; if you really want to do things in this business, you can. One of our most

successful businesses is run by somebody
who left school at sixteen, and it's very important to us to send out that signal. We
have thousands of people working in ware-
houses in the United States, doing quite
repetitive jobs. I always think that somewhere in there are people like our printers,
who, with an opportunity, could do great
things.

TAKEAWAYS

- ⚔ You're almost always wrong when you
  assume that people don't have ambition, can't do anything more than they
  are already doing, and really don't
  matter very much.

- ⚔ Understand what people would
  like to do and where you can give them
  a chance to unlock the talent that's

there, which sometimes doesn't get noticed.

⚟ It doesn't matter what your qualifications are; if you really want to do things in business, you can.

Adapt Your Leadership Style for Each Individual

David Brandon

*Chairman and CEO,
Domino's Pizza*

EARLY IN MY career, I worked for a great company, Procter & Gamble. I was with them for several years, and my earliest assignment was a very, very entry-level position where I was calling on grocery stores and selling them products, both in distribution and for merchandising purposes. Once you've served your tenure in that particular job, your hope would be to develop into a management position, and I was very fortunate that after a relatively short period of time I had proven what I needed to prove and was invited to become a manager. This was only a year and a half after I was out of school and very young. The realization hit me that I was going to wake up the next morning and I was actually going to have people who were reporting to me—I was truly the leader of a small organization.

I called my father to share with him the good news, but he is also my most wise counsel and a source of tremendous advice. I must admit I had a little bit of trepidation because my father never attended university; he was never a manager of a business. His career pursuits were very different from that—he was more of a skilled tradesperson. So, I called my father and said, "Dad, I got this great promotion. Starting tomorrow I'm going to be a manager. Do you have any advice for me? This is new territory for your young son."

He said, "Dave, I only have one piece of advice for you that hopefully will be useful. I think what you should do is find out how people want to be treated and treat them that way—and if you do that as a leader I think you'll be very successful."

That was the best advice I've ever gotten. One of the things buried in the point that my father made to me was the realization that all people are different and they respond differently to different types of coaching methods. In American business we often try to come up with the one-size-fits-all solution to everything, and the bigger the organization, the more inclined we are to issue some policy edict, procedure, or process that forces everybody to be put through the same channel in the way things are handled. I understand that. We certainly do that to the extent that it is necessary, but what my father taught me—and what I've learned—is that it's also very important to understand that people are individuals, and individuals react differently to different situations.

The best thing I can do to motivate some people who work for me is just to tell them how proud I am of them, how high my expectations are, and pat them on the head. They'll go out and perform at a higher level than you could ever imagine because, truthfully, they're going to put more pressure on themselves than I could ever put on them. There are other people who work for me, who, from time to time, need a little bit more encouragement. They need my direction. They need me to supply them with some reasons why they need to step it up and run a little harder and try a little more to achieve things. I think a good leader is someone who has the ability to assess the personality of an individual—what their wants, needs, and unique desires are—and adapt his leadership style in such a way that he appeals to the strengths and individual characteristics of that particular employee. It's the way to get the most out of them, and it's a way for them to be the most comfortable.

Motivating People

Another point that is related to this is the development of trust. If you don't develop trust among the people that you work with, all is lost. So, how do you get trust? One of the most important things about trust is to have a relationship that's based on both respect and, truthfully, a desire to work with one another and a desire to help one another be successful. I think what my dad was saying is that if I'm in a position where I can really understand how people want to be treated and treat them that way, they're going to respond with respect, they're going to trust me, and they're going to like me—because who doesn't want to be treated in that manner?

That leads me to my third point: a leader in any organization, particularly a large one, is only going to be as successful as their team wants them to be. If my team here at Domino's woke up one morning and said, "You know what? We've decided that Dave doesn't deserve to be successful, and we're going to start doing things that are going to undermine his ability to be successful," I would fail. There's no leader in the world who's powerful enough to overcome a team that doesn't really believe in them and want them to be successful.

So, my lesson in life and in business has been to create a circumstance where the people I call upon to do work on my behalf and create results on my behalf respect me. I need them to trust me. To earn that respect and trust, I need them to know that I'm going to treat them in a manner that's very consistent with the way they want to be treated.

TAKEAWAYS

⚔ It's very important to understand that people are individuals, and individuals react differently to different situations.

Motivating People

- Adapting your leadership style in such a way that you appeal to the strengths and individual characteristics of employees is the way to get the most out of them and a way for them to be the most comfortable.

- A leader is only going to be as successful as his team wants him to be.

———◆◆◆———

Getting the Best Out of a Diverse Team

———◆◆◆———

Clive Mather

Former President and CEO, Shell Canada

DIVERSITY ITSELF IS fascinating but not necessarily productive. Diversity can simply lead to disagreement or conflict. You need time to understand why people think differently and to then actually translate that into something effective.

Motivating People

I go back to Gabon, French-speaking
West Africa in the early 1980s, where I spent
four years with my family on the coast in the
tropical rainforests. In West Africa you have
amazing diversity of flora and fauna—as
much as you would find in the Amazon. It is
a rich, rich environment, and it was the
same at work. We had many tribes and of
course a predominantly black workforce,
but quite a number of expatriates from different countries. Women were much valued
in that African society, probably even more
there than they were in Europe at that time.

If I think about the team with which I
worked back in the early 1980s, it was indeed diverse: different creeds, different
cultures, different tribes, and so on. Did it
all work wonderfully well? I think it did, but
it was hard work. If you want to really harness the impact of diversity, it takes a lot of
effort. If I am honest, if I think back to perhaps a year after I had arrived, I really won-
dered whether I would actually get this rich
team to work. A bit like being in the jungle,

it seemed to make a lot of noise, but I wasn't sure exactly where the harmony was. By the time I left, it had changed a lot. I suspect I had changed a lot, too. What I really learned was that it takes effort to build an inclusive environment in which you can really harness the diversity of all the people around you.

To build inclusiveness, you first need a very simple but profound respect for individuals. A group may be diverse, but each one of us is just *us*. We are unique; we are ourselves, and that has to be recognized. A leader in any team must start with that simple recognition of individuals.

From there it's about finding time for the team to work together around issues, which gradually, over time, become more challenging. So, start with tasks; start with problems that quickly resonate with the team so that you can build understanding, you can build relationships, and you can build trust. As you do that, the capacity of the team to leverage all the different, unique perspectives grows. And what starts perhaps as a cacophony does indeed end in a harmony. Then diversity really starts to kick in because people now bring their perspectives and different opinions to really make for a richness that can enable you to work faster, smarter, and certainly to think of solutions which otherwise would never have been within the framework of that team.

What I learned—and I go back to my African experience, but it's generally, too—is that if you want to derive business value from diversity—if you really want to make an impact to your bottom line—it requires time and effort. Make it part of your personal agenda as a leader. Be clear to people about your respect for individuals and encourage all of those around you to do the same. That's how you create new solutions to old problems; that's how you learn to work smarter; and that's how you benefit the bottom line of your organization.

TAKEAWAYS

⚔ It takes effort to build an inclusive environment in which you can harness the diversity of all the people around you.

⚔ To build inclusiveness, you first need a very simple but profound respect for individuals.

⚔ If you start with tasks and problems that quickly resonate with the team in order to build understanding, relationships, and trust, the capacity of the team to leverage all its different, unique perspectives grows.

Instilling Belief in an Underperforming Sales Team

Charles Brewer

*Senior Vice President and General Manager
for the Northeast Region, DHL Express*

WHETHER YOU HAVE ten salespeople or
a thousand salespeople—selling pens,
pencils, icebergs, or whatever it may
be—they're actually selling through their

Instilling Belief

organization. Selling is about passion and belief. The salesman in question has to go out Monday through Friday completely convinced, passionate, and enthusiastic to sell the product that he's actually selling. On many occasions I've seen examples of great sales teams, people, managers, and leaders who've slightly missed the point in terms of what the sales organization was trying to do and what those salespeople should have been trying to do on a daily basis.

One good example of that would be some ten years ago when I was in the London area. I inherited a sales team, about two hundred salespeople. Because of some new entrants into the market, a previously very successful sales area was actually on the decline and not performing particularly well. In the first few days of being in that role, it was clear that it wasn't a case that people weren't right, or indeed, that the product was wrong. It was about passion and belief. They were on the back foot; they were defending their customers and not going on the offensive and taking a share from the competition.

Motivating People

From day one we got the sales organization together and reestablished the purpose of that group; a lot of rah-rah, a lot of motivation, a lot of morale. We set the goals very clearly, articulated those goals, and made sure they clearly understood what we were trying to do. Then we built the measures around that to make sure we could track on a daily basis what we were doing. That in itself doesn't really cut it.

The second part of that is then looking at your product portfolio. In my organization we had a great product portfolio, but we had to look for those differentiation points, and they're different depending on which markets you work in. So, with the sales organization, in the first few weeks of being there, we identified very quickly what they felt were the key things we needed to do. Perhaps that was where we had lost some of our focus, from the product perspective, and they were very quick to tell me where they felt we needed to go in terms of differentiation.

Having established that, we set up a six-point plan from the product perspective and put it in place. Now the salespeople understood what they had to do, they were motivated to want to do it, and they had a briefcase of differentiated product structures they could take to market. In a twelve-month period, that business unit went from a negative position to becoming the fastest growing business unit in the U.K. It was a great example of clear, one-on-one sales leadership.

The second example was in a very different market. It was in Asia; it was in the Philippines. Again, going into that environment, our sales organization—about one hundred and ten people—was not the market leader, so it was a very different challenge, a different set of business rules.

The market leader had a very strong and solid platform to sell from. Probably from a price perspective they were a little bit better than our company. From our perspective it was somewhat difficult for us to compete from a purely economic basis, so clearly just working down through one line of the sales process wasn't going to achieve very much.

Again, it was interesting, and in the same way, in the first few weeks, we sat down and did a lot of listening: listening to what the salespeople were saying, listening to what the customers were saying, and we spent a lot of time actually out in the major markets, understanding what the customers were saying wasn't right in our product portfolio or, indeed, in our sales delivery. A lot of it was about sales delivery—seeing what wasn't right—and then we set about creating that strategy.

The turning point, which was fantastic, was very simple. We got the one hundred and ten salespeople in a restaurant, a very nice restaurant in downtown Manila, and we needed to give them an icon, something to latch on to. Given that we were the underdog, and very much the underdog in that market, we came up with the idea that what they needed was to get their roar back, to get their lion's roar: to go on the offensive.

If salespeople spend their whole time thinking, "We're the underdog, and we can't compete in this marketplace," they're not going to sell anything. We need to make them believe, really believe, that they can take their product to the market, go on the offensive, and take away share from the very strong leading competitor.

So, at the evening's event, I dressed as a lion and came onstage, and the marketing manager at the time told the story about how the lion got its roar back. The story lasted about five or ten minutes, culminating in the end with this whole sales organization creating the roar.

Now in itself, it sounds really simple, but sales management is real, 101, simple stuff. From that day forward, every single day, we used that icon of a lion every time we had a success, no matter how small it was, to say, "There's the roar. There's the roar of our organization."

Every salesperson, from the smallest channel—telephone sales—to our national customers, started to believe that he really could sell the products. In exactly the same way as we had the success in the U.K., from being the worst-performing business unit in the Asia-Pacific region, we became the second best-performing business unit in the Asia-Pacific region, which was really some going in a market where we were clearly number three.

In summary there are three things I would share, and those taught me very good lessons. I also learned some things I wouldn't do again. Perhaps I wouldn't dress up as a lion again; I hated that. But I have three very positive stories. One is that sales-people need clarity of focus: What am I try-ing to do? What do you as an organization want me to do? Where am I going?

The second one is, it doesn't matter whether it's a team of one hundred people, a team of two hundred people or, here where I am in the U.S., a team of eleven hundred salespeople, they all need clear guidance and real belief in what they're sell-ing. You get that belief across by leading from the front, by being out with them, telling them what's right, telling them what they need to do, supporting them on the sales call, and giving them motivation to go and sell the product.

Instilling Belief

The third thing is, no matter what scenario you're in, whether you're number one, two, three, four, five, and on to however many competitors play in your space, it's not about necessarily moving from fifth to first, or fourth to third, or second to first. It's about making incremental gains and celebrating every single opportunity you get to close those small gains. In those scenarios we took great opportunities to celebrate every single win, from the smallest to the very largest. Trust me, nothing breeds success like success. If you celebrate every single opportunity, that ball starts rolling, and it starts moving in the right direction.

TAKEAWAYS

- ⚔ Analyzing and identifying key differentiators within your product portfolio for each of its different markets is a

powerful step in enabling the success
of your sales team.

-⚔ Salespeople need clarity of focus that
comes from asking: What am I trying
to do? What does my organization
want me to do? Where am I going?

-⚔ Regardless of a team's size, every salesperson within it needs clear guidance
and real belief in what he or she is
selling.

-⚔ Nothing breeds success like success,
which is all about making incremental
gains and celebrating every single gain
you make.

Recognize That Talent Is the Scarce Resource

Shelly Lazarus

Chairman and CEO, Ogilvy & Mather Worldwide

THE THING THAT I've come to learn and to know, through more than thirty years in the advertising industry and in running an advertising agency, is that it's all about people. If you just focus on people, everything else

good happens from that. We have a saying
around here: the people with the best
people win.

I remember when I was first named
CEO—I hadn't taken the job yet actually—I
asked if I could go and visit David Ogilvy,
who was the founder of this agency. I went
to see him for three days in Touffou, his
chateau in France. He was retired, but he
still had influence on the agency. I spent
three days with him. I remember it was sort
of dark and cold and windy, and so we stayed
inside. All we did was talk, for three days. I
kept asking him if there was anything he
could do differently, if there were any words
of advice that he could give me as I was taking on the leadership of this agency.

He kept saying to me, "It's so simple. All
you have to do is worry about the people.
When you recruit the best people, when you
create an atmosphere where they can be successful, where they can grow, where they're
nurtured, everything else will follow that."
And thinking back, David said about him-
self, "As much as I knew that, when I was

running the agency, as much as I believed it, as much time as I spent with the people in the company, it wasn't enough time. Unless I was spending 100 percent of the time with the people, it wasn't enough time."

So, how do you really take care of your people? It's a thing that's really easy to say. Everyone says it. And yet, I think there aren't that many organizations that truly care about individuals.

The first thing is that you have to judge people based on how they develop their people. You can have great financial success, but if the people who are working for you are leaving, that's a desperate failure in our company. So, people are truly judged by their ability to develop people and to keep them and to make them successful. I also think it requires a great deal of flexibility. Hard-drawn rules about what people are allowed to do in a company or how they are treated, I think, don't work. I've often felt that, in prior years, the organization told the individual what to do, and that the individual had to adapt to the organization.

In modern thinking the organization has to adapt to the individual.

Talent is the scarce resource. And once you recognize that, it is amazing how adaptable a large organization can be to an individual's needs. I learned this lesson very early on myself—and it's probably the reason I'm still at Ogilvy. I had some trouble with my first pregnancy, and I decided to come back to work, against doctor's orders. I hadn't been back in the office for more than three hours—I was an account executive at the time; I was a child—when the telephone rang. It was the president of the agency, who said, "I know you're back. I know what's going on. I don't approve of the fact that you've gotten out of bed and come back, but so be it." He said, "But the least I can do is send my car to pick you up every morning and have it for you to go home at night, because that's the only way I can feel okay about you doing this."

I never forgot it. It's probably the reason that I'm still at Ogilvy today. It wasn't even so much the car, but the fact that he knew, that he cared enough to do something about it, and then that he actually took the action. Every day of my life leading Ogilvy, I try to replicate the car experience, to see whether I can figure out those things that will make the most difference to the lives overall of the people I care about who work for this company.

TAKEAWAYS

◄ When you recruit the best people, when you create an atmosphere where they can be successful, where they can grow, and where they're nurtured, everything good will follow.

◄ Flexibility works much better than hard-drawn rules about what people

are allowed to do or how they are
treated in a company.

✠ Once you recognize that talent is the
scarce resource, it is amazing how
adaptable a large organization can be
to an individual's needs.

Looking After Your People

Philip Williamson

Former Chief Executive, Nationwide Building Society

I CAME FROM a relatively humble background. My parents were "working class," and nobody in our family had ever been to grammar school before, or anything of that nature. I learned a lot from my father in particular because he invested a great deal of time in me.

Something that sticks in my mind was when I first went to grammar school; I was

picked to play for the cricket team. We
didn't have a lot of money as a family,
and I didn't have cricket boots. I used to
have white pumps. And the cricket master
said to me, "Philip, we'd like you to be in
the team, but you have to have some cricket
boots." So, my father had to go and work
overtime to buy me a pair of cricket boots,
and that's quite a commitment in people, in
me—obviously, with blood relatives it's
slightly different—but even so, I remember
that particular story well and with a great
deal of affection because I think it's very
unselfish behavior. My parents were very
generous and giving people, and they invested in me. And that's something in business life that I believe very strongly in.

So, now I am very keen to invest in Nationwide's people, because I genuinely believe you tend to get out of things what you
put into them. In my early life, my father
invested in me, that is for sure. And I think
in my early career as well, people have invested in me. They've shown a commitment
to my performance. One general manager

Looking After Your People

I worked with, when I was working at Lloyds
Bank as a relatively junior personal assistant
to the general managers—I remember this
story quite clearly—phoned me up one day
and said, "Philip, have you got a minute?"
I went down to his room, had a chat with
him. I'd just produced a response to a complaint letter—because the complaint letters
used to come forward to the general managers. He sat me down and said, "By the way,
Philip, I'd just like you to know something.
I honestly could not have written that letter
better myself." That's quite a humbling experience when a very senior guy—and I was
a very junior manager—brought me out of
the way just to say, "Good job. Well done.
Thank you."

I think it is important that people feel
that other people are sincerely interested in
them. They feel it emotionally. We did some
research that proved quite categorically that
there is a very distinct correlation between
the way people feel about working for your
company and their actual business performance over time. So, we basically spent a

lot of time investing, coaching, training—
working very hard on our people equation—
to make sure that we had the right people
with the right skills and the right attitudes
and values to make things happen at the end
of the day. And that's how it's worked.
They've paid us back big time.

We have a whole series of recognition initiatives, and celebration is very important in
the organization. One of the things I intro-
duced when I was first made chief executive
was something that we call PRIDE. PRIDE is
a mnemonic; it stands for: Putting members first, Rising to the challenge, Inspiring
confidence, Delivering best value, Exceed-
ing expectations. It's our brand; it's the way
we do things—our attitudes, our behaviors,
the things that make Nationwide what it is
today. And when people do really good
things, we give them a PRIDE certificate or a
PRIDE award. Or we give them a red letter
day or something of that nature, all sorts of
recognition initiatives of one type or another, so that they realize how important
they are as individuals.

Looking After Your People

So, investing in people, recognizing people, just basically looking after those people pays back big time in business results at the end of the day.

TAKEAWAYS

- ⚔ There is a distinct correlation between the way people feel about working for a company and their actual business performance over time.

- ⚔ Recognition initiatives and celebrations are important demonstrations to employees that they are individually valued and appreciated.

- ⚔ Investing in people, recognizing people, and looking after those people pays back big time in business results.

Leadership Is About Empowering Others to Lead

William George

Former Chairman and CEO, Medtronic, Inc.

WHEN I WAS a young person, I used to read books on great leaders, and I developed this philosophy of trying to be one of those great leaders. We thought in those days that leadership was following the great man over the hill—most of them were men coming out of two world wars and a depression; people like General George Patton—in spite of all their flaws and negative characteristics. I think we finally realized in the twenty-first century that leadership is not about following someone else. It's not about having power over other people. It's about empowering people to step up and lead.

Everyone says, "Where have all the leaders gone?" That's because they're looking for the perfect leader. There are no perfect leaders. Certainly, I was anything but perfect. But what they do have is leaders who empower other people. Look at the great leaders in business today. For example, the CEO of Avon Products, Andrea Jung, has 5.5 million people working for her; she's incredibly empowering. Anne Mulcahy of Xerox. Jeff Immelt at GE. Sam Palmisano at IBM. A.G. Lafley at Procter & Gamble. These kinds of leaders realize they need thousands, maybe tens of thousands of leaders inside their own companies, and they empower people to step up and take the lead. And that's how they get much more out of people, get them to be much more creative, much more committed. Because when you're empowered, you're committed.

When I first went to Medtronic, I was talking about empowerment a lot. And people said, "It's not very empowering when you ask us all these tough questions."

I said, "It's really those tough questions that are allowing us to perform. And one of the keys is, are you going to fulfill your responsibilities?"

They said, "Oh, you're talking about empowerment with responsibilities," to which I said, "Is there any other kind?"

Empowerment does assume responsibility. I have the power, and I'm going to be empowered to go make a difference. Empowered leaders are the key to restoring trust in leadership and building more leaders, because if we can empower people at a young age to take the lead, we can transform organizations and get thousands of people to lead.

I'll give you an example of a woman whom I once visited in a Medtronic facility that made heart valves. She was carving up pigs' valves and making them into heart valves. I visited her bench because the company was heavily backlogged and she was the highest producer in the facility. I said, "Tell me about your work."

She wouldn't even look down at her bench; she wanted to look up. And with passion in her eyes, she said, "Mr. George, let me tell you what I do. I make heart valves that save people's lives, and I sign off on these valves. There are no inspectors on this line. Before I'll sign my name on that valve, I put it through the test. Is it good enough for my father? Is it good enough for my husband? How about my daughter? And if it passes those tests, then it goes out of here. I make a thousand valves a year, and if one of those valves is defective, someone's going to die. And maybe to you 99.9 percent quality is good enough, but I can tell you, I could never live with that on my conscience. But when I go home at night, what I think about are five thousand people who are alive today because of the heart valves I made."

Now, that woman's a leader. She has
no direct report, but she's an empowered
leader. She's a role model for everyone else
in that facility. Everyone's trying to emulate
her and her kind of work.

It's that kind of empowerment that
enables people to make a difference in their
work and to inspire others to do likewise.
This is good in any industry. I've seen people like this in the oil and gas industry, in
the pharmaceutical industry, in the banking
industry; it doesn't really matter. The question is, do you feel the power to make a
difference through your work and have a
purpose for that work which brings people
together around a sense of "we can come
together and we can make a difference"?

TAKEAWAYS

⚍ The great leaders in business realize
   they need thousands of leaders inside

their own companies, and they empower people to step up and take the lead.

⧓ Empowerment assumes responsibility.

⧓ It is important that employees feel they possess the power to make a difference through their work and have a purpose for that work which brings people together.

Leading People Through Change

Amy Butte

Former Chief Financial Officer, MF Group

I ARRIVED AT the New York Stock Exchange in January of 2004. The first day that I arrived, I went and I met the finance department. Now, when I envisioned being a part of the New York Stock Exchange and being CFO of the exchange, I will admit that I envisioned probably more glamorous things. What I didn't envision—and what ironically turned into probably the most satisfying part of the job——is the transformation that took place within the finance department itself.

So, on my first day, I go and meet the finance department. And there are about sixty-five people in the finance department. They're in a building not connected to the executive floor of the exchange; it's called 20 Broad. When I walk in on the first day, there are just boxes and boxes of paper, floor to ceiling. I'm thinking, "This is the New York Stock Exchange. This is all about technology and paperless trading." That's how I grew up. That's how I learned the business.

While I was meeting with the people, I asked them a basic question. I asked, "How do you perceive yourself, or how do you think the exchange perceives the finance department?"

And they said, "We're not important. We're viewed as people who process numbers, push paper——but we're not important."

Motivating People

I set off to create a transformation effort within the finance function. The strategy was to become a strategic partner under the organization to create a system that was based on three primary objectives: transparency, processing control, and efficiency. To do that we really needed to pull three levers. We needed to change our technology infrastructure, the organizational alignment, and a lot of the processes that we had within the organization. It was a complete overhaul. The number of changes was just tremendous.

I spent time working with the group to create a mantra, which was, "We make a difference." We held workshops through the year. I tried to spend time on the floor getting to know people, have open-office hours, set up training modules, and make them feel that they were important because they were important to getting all of that changed. If they hadn't changed their mindset, there's no way that we would have been able to accomplish as much as we did.

Leading People Through Change

A good example of changing the mindset was Doreen, who had been in collections for twenty-six years. I promoted her to head of collections. I remember seeing her one day about two months after she had been promoted, and she was all smiling and proud of herself. I asked, "What are you doing today, Doreen?" And she said, "Oh, we're changing our exception report. We're running it differently, and we found some accounts that we hadn't really paid attention to before because we'd been running it the same way for about five years." Just because she had been given the opportunity to lead the group, she was thinking differently, and that was making a difference.

There's a gentleman who was an assistant controller and is now our treasurer, whose whole life has changed. His whole demeanor has changed. He has been able to do things that he never was able to do, and here he was putting in a cash management system, negotiating our insurance, and managing a $1 billion portfolio with external advisers. This person's whole life has changed.

And other people in the department saw that. One woman was named assistant controller after being there for twenty-nine years. I saw her one day, and she was smiling. I asked, "What are you laughing about?"

And she said, "Well, I was asked what I'm going to say when I retire." She's retiring in January. "You know, I think I know what I'm going to say. I've been here for thirty years, and the last year was the most fun."

Leading people through change is not that easy. At first there will be a great deal of resistance to what you're doing, and it's important to create a mission, to create a statement. Our goal was to become a strategic partner, and we had a path to get there.

Second, no matter how great the vision or how important the need, unless you get the buy-in of the people within the organization, you're never going to get there because you can't do it yourself.

And third, you can find success in unexpected places. For me, on a personal level, I found success in being a part of the change that happened to the individuals within the finance department as much as in the strategic success—the sexy success, if you will—that was part of the broader organization. The case studies don't tell you about people and how you impact their lives every day when they come into work. The average tenure at the exchange is twenty years, so when you're doing things differently because there are different systems, different processes, and different philosophies, that's going to be the most transformational part of it. And if you can't get people to change, if you can't get your own department to buy into it, you're never going to be successful within the rest of the organization.

TAKEAWAYS

⊰ In order to overcome resistance to change, it's important to create a mission and a clear path to your goal.

Motivating People

⚐ No matter how great the vision or how important the need for a change, without buy-in from the people within the organization, you'll never achieve it because you can't do it yourself.

⚐ You can find success in unexpected places.

———◆———

Respect and Value Every Individual's Contribution

———◆———

Amelia Fawcett

Former Vice Chairman and Chief Operating Officer,
Morgan Stanley International

IN ANY ORGANIZATION, every individual has
something to contribute.

I remember being a young student in
secondary school working for a law firm in

Motivating People

Boston. I really was at the low end of the totem pole; I did bookkeeping, bookbinding, wiping the floor, photocopying—it didn't matter. In a firm of highly professional individuals I was about as low as it got. What impressed me was that one or two very talented senior partners took an interest in what I did and took the time to explain to me why what I did was important to them and the firm. To this day, many years later, I can remember the sense of pride and enthusiasm for what I did because they took pride and enthusiasm in my actions and clearly valued my contribution.

More recently, I had the great privilege of being the guest of the admiral of the U.S. fleet in the Mediterranean, along with the then U.S. ambassador to the U.K. and several CEOs. We spent the weekend on the USS *Enterprise* and over those two days we met people and saw initiatives going on from stem to stern, top to bottom, everywhere on that aircraft carrier. What struck me the most was standing on the bridge at night, looking down on the deck and seeing the

planes landing and taking off, as well as all
the different individuals who made sure that
it all happened safely. They were wearing
different colored fluorescent jackets, depending on their team, and looked like bees
flying around the deck. It was very clear that
each one had a role and if one didn't do his
job properly, someone could die. It made a
very big impression on me.

I don't want to suggest that financial services firms are like aircraft carriers; we're
certainly not in the business of life-and-
death situations. But the concept that every
individual has an important contribution to
make is the same. Whether you're a fighter
pilot or a banker, you need to understand
that it takes an entire team to get those
planes on and off the deck carefully, just as
it takes an entire team to make sure that se-
curities are traded and deals are done.

That's sometimes a difficult thing
for a very highly motivated, powerful,
successful banker to understand about the
infrastructure of a team. One of the key
roles that senior management has is to be on

that bridge; they can see the entire picture
and how all the different parts need to fit
together. It's their role to find that balance;
to encourage people to perform to their
highest potential and to recognize that all
contributions are highly valued and absolutely integral to the success of the whole.

So, I think it is critically important that
management takes the responsibility because
they are best placed to ensure that every
player is a player, performs to his full potential, and understands everybody else's
value. At the end of the day, we need to show
respect for each other and for the contribution that everyone makes because people
who work for us look to us for leadership.
If our standards are any different to the
standards we ask of them, then we really
don't have a right to expect them to behave
any differently. In the language of change,
you need to walk the talk.

You need to start by respecting the contribution and work that everybody does and
then encourage your team to understand
that to get those planes off the deck and get

them back on safely everybody has to work together seamlessly. In an era where there are no easy answers and no silver bullets, you need to harness the talents of every individual if you're going to service your clients, find innovative solutions, and grow your business.

TAKEAWAYS

⚵ One of the key roles of senior management is to find the right balance among employee talents, to encourage people to perform to their highest potential, and to recognize that all contributions are highly valued and absolutely integral to the success of the whole.

⚵ If a leader's standards are different from the standards she asks of employees, then she really doesn't have a right to expect them to behave any differently.

⚑ In an era where there are no easy answers and no silver bullets, leaders need to harness the talents of every individual if they're going to service clients, find innovative solutions, and grow the business.

Staging
Significant
Moments

Jay Conger

Henry Kravis Research Chair Professor,
Kravis Leadership Institute

THIS LESSON IS about the fact that you as a leader can actually stage events—I call them significant moments—which you use to realign the organization. In essence, you're saying to the organization, through this event, that something's different in our world now, and we need to move our focus or we need to change an aspect of who we are in order to adapt to a changing environment.

The example of a significant moment that's one of my personal favorites is set in the mid-nineties at ASDA in the United Kingdom, which was a very well-established grocery store chain that had built its success around a low-cost, high-volume grocery model. It was an organization that had basically had too much success, so that after a few decades it became very insular. It lost its way; it lost its markets. And in 1995 it actually sat on the edge of bankruptcy. The board, in a moment of desperation, before actually watching this organization literally crumble, brought in two outsiders to save the organization, one of whom was Allan Leighton, who was the chief operating officer.

What Allan did in his first week at ASDA was spend the first few days out in the stores, meeting with store managers, employees, and customers to assess what had gone wrong. In the middle of the week, he staged a significant moment. He called in the top management of ASDA, the existing management team. He invited them into a conference room, and there he was at the front of the room. He greeted them, and, of course, he was the new boss. What they first noticed was that he was not wearing his jacket, which was a bit unusual in the ASDA culture—it was a more formal culture.

After greeting them, he said, "Now here's what I'd like us to do. I'm going to give each of you a coat hanger, and I'm going to ask that you take off your jacket because what's happening with this organization is that we've lost touch with our stores. We've lost touch with our customers. And in many ways, our formality and distance has brought that about. Now you'll notice on the coat hangers I'm giving each of you, which I'm hoping you'll hang your jacket on, is that it says 'No jacket required.' That's the future; because I need us all to get back out and talk to our customers, talk to our managers and employees."

Motivating People

He continued, "In addition, what I'm going to do is give you this rather large ten-foot-long ruler." At that moment, in the room appeared literally dozens of these enormous rulers, and with a smile, he said, "Now, Wal-Mart in the United States has this very simple idea, and that is, whenever a customer is within ten feet of you, you go and you talk to the customer. And what I'm going to ask us to do over the intervening months ahead is to reach out, talk to our customers, get back in touch with our market. So you'll have this ten-foot ruler, and whenever you whack a customer by accident, carrying it around, you'll be forced to go and talk to them."

After handing out these two mementos or, I would argue, symbols, of the coat hanger with "No jacket required" and the ten-foot ruler, Allan then asked everybody to stand up and in a playful pledge head out to the stores and reinvent ASDA. It's a very wonderful moment because what you see as you watch this moment is that two-thirds of the group are amazed and engaged. It's almost like a breath of fresh air comes into the organization, a chance to reinvigorate the organization and then, literally, to save it. There is a smaller group that finds this quite threatening and intimidating, and what you see when you watch the actual video of this moment, is that that group kept their jackets on. In many ways it's a very wonderful moment for Allan because he's actually able to assess potentially who is with him and who is not with him.

The point is that you and I can stage simple events to send a message around priorities that are emerging, that require a change in approach or a change in behavior. What Allan was striving to do through this moment was alter the culture of the top team, which was a culture built around entitlement and, in many ways, distance from the very people they served. He wanted them to get back out and touch back into the world that was their lifeblood: the stores and the people who came to the stores.

Think about what your highest priority is that demands some type of change in the minds and behaviors of your staff. Put it on a stage through a very simple event, and if you can, attach a symbol to it, so everybody will remember what's important to do after the event. In yourself, model the very behavior you're asking people to do in your event.

So, we go back to the story of ASDA and how Allan spent the first few days in the store, talking to managers, employees, and customers: what he was about to ask his team to do. And in the significant moment, he's got his jacket off as a model of what he's going to ask you to do. It's very important in these moments to be consistent in your own behavior with what you're going to ask others to do.

TAKEAWAYS

⊰ Leaders can stage events—significant moments—to realign an organization

Staging Significant Moments

by communicating through the event that the company needs to adapt to a changing environment.

⚔ Before staging the event, determine what type of change in the minds and behaviors of your staff is of highest priority, put it on a stage through a simple event, and if you can, attach a symbol to it so those present will remember what's important.

⚔ It's important in staging significant moments to be consistent in your own behavior with what you're going to ask others to do.

Passion

Perween Warsi

Founder and CEO, S&A Foods

IT'S VERY IMPORTANT to have passion for your business and for the products you sell. Be proud of your business and encourage your people to be proud that they are producing good quality products. Ensure that they have confidence in themselves to do their jobs. People matter so much; the business is not bricks and mortar, it is people.

We have taste panels every day to release our products, but I personally get involved

Passion

with the Tuesday morning panel because I am very passionate about quality. We invite people from throughout the chain, so we will have prep people, cooks, people from the filling room, the line-setters, and departmental managers. Everybody understands the high standard of quality that's expected from us as a supplier. We want to be proud of selling our products. You can tell when they talk about it: they talk with so much passion. If you have that in people, you don't have to go and tell them what to do about it because they'll do it for you.

Once, we were due to have a visit from a customer the next day, and I only found out about it at 4:30 that Monday afternoon. I picked up the phone and rang my chef and said, "We've got this customer visit; what are we going to do about it? What are we sampling?"

They had prepared, but they had not prepared the things that I felt that we should be sampling. I had a chat with him and said, "Look, this is a good opportunity, and we should sample this, that, and the other."

Motivating People

He could tell that I was really passionate about it and that I really wanted to excite my customers.

He said, "Even if I have to come in at five o'clock in the morning to do those products, I will. Leave it with me, and I'll sort it out."

The next morning, the customer visit was at 10 a.m., with lunch at 11 a.m., and when I went to the development kitchen the whole table was laid out with a fantastic range of food. The chef had done it because he believed that it was very important and because he was proud of doing it.

When I first set up the business, I had five ladies helping me, and it was very easy because we talked to each other. But when you have a thousand people working in the business it's extremely difficult. I can't do it on my own. I need every single one of my team to share the passion and to convey the same passion to everybody else on the factory floor.

If you win the hearts and minds of people: if you train them, develop them, give them the confidence to feel good about what they do and to take pride in it, that's the magic. And it works because you're dealing with people.

TAKEAWAYS

꙰ If you instill passion in people for their product or service, you don't have to tell them what to do about it because they'll do it for you.

꙰ A leader needs every single one of her team members to share her passion and to convey that same passion to everybody else in the organization; she cannot do it alone.

꙰ If you win the hearts and minds of people: if you train them, develop them, give them the confidence to feel

Motivating People

good about what they do and to take
pride in it, that's the magic. And it
works because you're dealing with
people.

The Power of Good Conversation

Lynda Gratton

*Professor of Management Practice,
London Business School*

FOR YEARS ONE of the things I've really tried to do is encourage the financial community to think about human capital when they come to value an organization, because at the moment there isn't really any agreed way of putting human capital on the balance sheet. In many ways that's right and proper. But the leading-edge research I did over ten years showed that some leaders were systematically destroying the human capital of their organization: they were destroying commitment, they were destroying engagement. Yet it was very difficult for the financial community to understand that until long after the capital had been destroyed.

For some years now, I've been encouraging analysts to think about human capital. And one of the ways that I did that—and for me it was just a huge lesson—is that I talked to a bunch of some of the most gifted analysts in the world. I said to them, "I wonder if it's going to be possible for you to go into an organization and to understand that organization from the perspective of the people, rather than from the perspective of the finance?" I said, "Think about it like the smell of the place. You know: when you go into a restaurant, you can tell almost instantly whether you like this place. Some places smell fabulous—you feel great. Some feel really dreadful."

We took this group of analysts on an enormous bus around California, and we looked at companies such as eBay and Palm—loads and loads of different companies. I said to them, "Please don't ask any questions about the financials of these companies; just observe and listen and see if you can get the smell of the place." And what was really fascinating was that within a very short period of time they had learned how to use those senses that they had to identify whether an organization was exciting, whether people were energized, and whether it was full of potential.

Of course, the interesting thing was that they then began to see those companies in different ways. One of the things that they noticed—and I began to notice as well—is the sort of conversations that were going on. So, for example, we'd go into one organization and it seemed to be that as we walked

around everybody was running around,
everyone seemed to be on mobile phones;
there didn't seem to be any sort of real conversations going on. In other organizations
we saw that people were talking to each other
really carefully.

At that stage I learned about the power of
good conversation. And since that time I've
thought and written about conversation
quite a lot. It seems to me that organizations
that have great conversations realize very
powerful conversations are not simply about
facts and data—they're also conversations
where people's emotions are part of the
conversation. In a sense people bring their
whole selves to the conversation; they're very
authentic about themselves.

What I also learned is that so many of us
in organizations are completely bewitched
by our agendas. We're so busy running
about, we just never give ourselves time to
have conversations with other people—to
actually sit and spend time with other people, talking about things that are important.

The Power of Good Conversation

And what I've learned is that great companies value that. One of the ways that they value it is to have CEOs or senior people who themselves engage in conversation. Senior people who have conversations with each other are basically giving other people in the organization permission to make space to have conversations. The CEO who runs around with a mobile phone attached to his ear the whole time is basically disempowering the possibility of people having conversations.

The way that an executive behaves, a senior executive in particular, sends very strong messages to the people around them about what's important and about what's valued in that organization. What I've seen is that chief executives and senior executives who are prepared and able to have deep, meaningful, purposeful conversations set up very powerful role models to people around them about what's valued in that organization and how they themselves can converse with other people.

TAKEAWAYS

- ⚔ The most powerful conversations are not simply about facts and data—they also include people's emotions and allow people to engage with their whole, authentic selves.

- ⚔ Great companies value conversations—people sitting and spending time together, talking about things that are important.

- ⚔ Senior executives who are able to have deep, meaningful, purposeful conversations set up powerful role models to people around them about what's valued in their organization and how they themselves can converse with others.

———◆◆◆———

Be Ambitious, Then Celebrate Your Success

———◆◆◆———

Mary Cantando

Founder, WomanBusinessOwner.com

NO MATTER WHAT, if something is really important to you, I find that you just have to overcome any excuses you have and figure out a way to make it happen.

As a teenager growing up in Philadelphia in the late sixties, I was offered several college scholarships, but I decided to go to work right after high school. It wasn't until I was about twenty-eight or twenty-nine years old that it dawned on me I had made a tragic mistake. Although I was very happy with my role as a wife and mother, and I had a great job, I still somehow always felt like a second-class citizen because I didn't have that college degree.

One day I was crying to my husband, John, about this feeling, and he said, "You know, Mary, you're twenty-nine years old. You can go back to school now and have your degree within ten years or less. Or you can moan about it, berate yourself, and end up being thirty-nine, and then forty-nine, and then fifty-nine, and still be in the same place." For my thirtieth birthday, I gave myself a present and went back to school.

My husband was on a fast-track corporate career, so there were a lot of bumps in the road. We lived in five cities by the time my youngest son was five years old, so I really struggled to get through. I remember the last semester—I had two courses left. It was a summer session where you had to go five days a week for three weeks. I had a 7 a.m. business law class, and I had a 7 p.m. philosophy class. So, I would leave my house before daybreak in the morning to drive downtown to Memphis to attend class, getting home around noon. Then after dinner, I'd head back down for my evening class, getting home about midnight. Those were three long weeks.

I finished my final business law exam and called my husband to tell him that I was going to go sell my book back and then zip down and meet him for breakfast. I'll never forget his words coming across the phone, "Sell the book? Sell the book? You go out to the quad and you spike that book!" John's words made me realize, first of all what I'd accomplished, but beyond that, the pure joy of celebrating a real accomplishment.

So, no matter what struggles I have come up against in business and in life, I look back to that five-year period and what I was able to accomplish and the obstacles that I overcame, and I'm always left with the sense that if I could do that, I could do anything. That has really carried me through my entire career.

I also look back on John's comment about spiking the book, and I look for opportunities to celebrate every success that I have—in business and in life—no matter how large or small.

TAKEAWAYS

⚔ If something is really important to you, you just have to overcome any excuses you have and figure out a way to make it happen.

⚔ The recollection of having overcome difficult obstacles in the past can be a powerful affirmation of strength and fortitude throughout one's career and life.

⚔ Look for opportunities to celebrate every success—in business and in life—no matter how large or small.

⊰ ABOUT THE ⊱ CONTRIBUTORS

Sir John Banham has been Chairman of Johnson Matthey since April 2006. He is also Chairman of Spacelabs Healthcare Inc., a Senior Independent Director of AMVESCAP and Cyclacel Pharmaceuticals, and a Director of Merchants Trust and of Invesco.

He started his career in the British Foreign Office in 1962 before moving to Reed International, where he became Director of Marketing. In 1969 he joined McKinsey and Company, becoming a Principal in 1975 and the youngest British director of the firm in 1980.

Sir John set up the Audit Commission in 1983 and was Director General of the Confederation of British Industry from 1987 to 1992.

He was the founding Chairman of Westcountry Television from the company's start-up in June 1992 until it was sold to Carlton Communications in December 1996. He then became Chairman of Kingfisher from 1996 to December 2001. Additionally, he was at the helm of Tarmac from February 1994 until March 2000.

Sir John was Chairman of Whitbread from 2000 to 2005 and also Chairman of Geest from 2002 to 2005.

About the Contributors

Sir David Bell is a Director of Pearson, an international media company.

He is also Chairman of the Financial Times Group, having been Chief Executive of the *Financial Times* since 1993.

In July 1998 Sir David was appointed Pearson's Director for People, with responsibility for the recruitment, motivation, development, and reward of employees across the Pearson Group. In addition, he is a Director of the *Economist*, the Vitec Group Plc, and the Windmill Partnership. Sir David is Chairman of Common Purpose International, Chairman of Crisis, Chairman of Sadler's Wells, and Chairman of the International Youth Foundation.

He was Chairman of the Millennium Bridge Trust (1995 to 2000), responsible for conceiving the first new bridge across the Thames in one hundred years.

Sir David was educated at Cambridge University and the University of Pennsylvania.

David Brandon is the Chairman and CEO of Domino's Pizza.

He started his career at Procter & Gamble, where he worked in sales management. In 1979, following his tenure at Procter & Gamble, he moved to Valassis Communications, Inc., a company in the sales promotion and coupon industries. He became President and Chief Executive Officer in 1989, a position he held until 1998, while additionally taking on the role of Chairman in his last two years there.

About the Contributors

Mr. Brandon subsequently moved to Domino's Pizza, and has been the company's Chairman and Chief Executive Officer since March 1999.

Charles Brewer is the Senior Vice President and General Manager for the Northeast Region, DHL Express, an express delivery and logistics company, a position he has held since December 2008.

Mr. Brewer has more than twenty-one years of industry experience at DHL. He was the Executive Vice President, Commercial, for DHL from November 2006 to December 2008 and Executive Vice President, U.S. Air Products and Services, from February through November 2006. Prior to that he managed country operations in Malaysia. Before his posting in Malaysia, he held senior positions in Asia Pacific and the United Kingdom.

Amy Butte is the former Chief Financial Officer of MF Group, a leading broker of exchange-listed futures and options.

Ms. Butte started her career in equity research at Merrill Lynch, and also worked at Bridge Trading Co. Inc., Merrin Financial, and Andersen Consulting.

Ms. Butte then moved to Bear Stearns & Co., Inc., where she became a Senior Managing Director in equity research, responsible for coverage of the brokerage, asset-gathering, and financial technology industries.

Following this, Ms. Butte became Chief Strategist and Chief Financial Officer with Credit Suisse

First Boston's financial services division. There she helped lead the development of the firm's global asset-gathering division and the sale of the firm's correspondent clearing business, Pershing, to the Bank of New York.

Ms. Butte joined the NYSE in February 2004 as Executive Vice President. She became Chief Financial Officer two months later. In this role she was responsible for all NYSE financial planning and operations. She stepped down as Chief Financial Officer of the NYSE in late 2006.

Ms. Butte joined Man Financial in August 2006 as Chief Financial Officer. In 2007, she became CFO and Director of MF Group, which formed when Man Financial announced it would spin off its brokerage unit. She stepped down from MF Group in 2008.

Ms. Butte is Cochairman of the New York City Ballet's Corporate Advisory Board and is an active member of the New York Women's Foundation.

Mary Cantando is the Founder of WomanBusiness Owner.com, a national advisory firm that focuses on helping women-owned businesses expand.

Ms. Cantando has more than twelve years of experience as an entrepreneurial executive and spent six years researching women business owners. She is a nationally recognized expert on growing women-owned businesses.

Ms. Cantando holds a seat on the National Board of the Women Presidents' Organization, an association of women who own multimillion-dollar businesses. She is also a member of the National Women's Forum, is certified by the Women's Business Enterprise National Council, and is a member of Women Impacting Public Policy.

Ms. Cantando is the author of *The Woman's Advantage: 20 Women Entrepreneurs Show You What It Takes to Grow Your Business* and *Nine Lives: Stories of Women Business Owners Landing on Their Feet*.

Jay Conger is the Henry Kravis Research Chair Professor of Leadership at the Kravis Leadership Institute at Claremont McKenna College.

Professor Conger is widely acknowledged as one of the world's experts on leadership. He has done extensive research into leadership, boards of directors, organizational change, and the training and development of leaders and managers.

Prior to his academic career Professor Conger worked in government and as an international marketing manager for a high-technology company.

After moving into academia, Professor Conger became a research scientist at the Center for Effective Organizations at the University of Southern California. He then became the Executive Director of its Leadership Institute.

Professor Conger was subsequently invited to join London Business School in 1999 in the role of Professor of Organizational Behavior. He remained there until he took his current position at Claremont McKenna College in 2005. Harvard Business School has also asked him to help redesign its organizational behavior course around leadership issues. Additionally, Professor Conger has been involved in executive education at INSEAD.

An accomplished writer, he has written or cowritten more than ten books and one hundred scholarly articles. His titles include *Shared Leadership: Reframing the How's and Why's of Leading Others* and *Winning 'Em Over: A New Model for Managing in the Age of Persuasion*. His latest book, *The Practice of Leadership: Developing the Next Generation of Leaders,* examines what top scholars consider the best practices of leadership in numerous sectors.

Alongside his academic work, Professor Conger consults for a number of private corporations and nonprofit organizations worldwide.

Amelia Fawcett is the former Vice Chairman and Chief Operating Officer of Morgan Stanley International. She is Chairman of Pensions First LLP, a financial services company launched in 2007 that aims to use the capital markets to tackle risks in U.K. final salary pension schemes.

Ms. Fawcett, a dual citizen of the United States and the United Kingdom, was with Morgan Stanley for twenty years, first joining the London office in 1987. She was then appointed Vice President in

1990, and Executive Director in 1992, moving up to the role of Managing Director and Chief Administrative Officer for the European operations in 1996. In 2002 she was appointed Vice Chairman of Morgan Stanley International, responsible for development and implementation of the company's business strategy. She left her position in September 2006.

Ms. Fawcett is Chairman of the National Portrait Gallery's Development Board, Chairman of the London International Festival of Theater, and a Director of State Street Corporation.

William George is the former CEO and chairman of Medtronic, Inc., a global leader in medical technology. He is currently Professor of Management Practice, Henry B. Arthur Fellow of Ethics, at Harvard Business School, a position he has held since 2004.

Mr. George received his BSIE from Georgia Institute of Technology in 1964 and his MBA from Harvard University in 1966. From 1966 to 1969, he worked in the U.S. Department of Defense as Special Assistant to the Secretary of the Navy and as Assistant to the Comptroller.

Thereafter, Mr. George served in executive positions at Litton Microwave Cooking Products from 1970 to 1978. From 1978 to 1989, Mr. George held a series of executive positions with Honeywell.

About the Contributors

In 1989 Mr. George joined Minneapolis-based Medtronic, Inc. as President and Chief Operating Officer, and from 1991 to 2001, he served as Chief Executive Officer. From 1996 to 2002, he was Medtronic's chairman. Under his leadership, Medtronic's market capitalization grew from $1.1 billion to $60 billion.

Mr. George has also served as Executive-in-Residence at Yale School of Management and Professor of Leadership and Governance at IMD International in Lausanne, Switzerland.

He is the author of *True North: Discover Your Authentic Leadership* and *Authentic Leadership: Rediscovering the Secrets to Creating Lasting Value*.

Mr. George currently serves as a Director of oil and gas giant ExxonMobil (since 2005) and investment banking firm Goldman Sachs & Co. (since 2002), as well as Carnegie Endowment for International Peace and World Economic Forum USA.

Lynda Gratton is the Professor of Management Practice at the London Business School. In this role she directs the school's executive program, Human Resource Strategy in Transforming Organizations. She is considered one of the world's authorities on people in organizations and actively advises companies across the world.

A trained psychologist, Professor Gratton worked for the global airline British Airways for several years as an occupational psychologist and then became Director of HR Strategy at PA Con-

sulting Group. From 1992 to 2002 she led the
Leading Edge Research Consortium.

Professor Gratton's book *Living Strategy*, originally
published in 2000, has been translated into more
than fifteen languages and rated by U.S. CEOs as
one of the most important books of the year. Her
more recent book, *The Democratic Enterprise*, was de-
scribed by the *Financial Times* as a work of important
scholarship. Her latest book, published in 2007, is
*Hot Spots: Why Some Teams, Workplaces, and Organizations Buzz
with Energy—and Others Don't*.

In 2005 Professor Gratton was appointed
the Director of the Lehman Centre for Women
in Business. In 2007 she was included in the
Times' list of the top fifty business thinkers in the
world.

Shelly Lazarus is the Chairman and CEO of
the International advertising, marketing,
and public relations agency Ogilvy & Mather
Worldwide.

Ms. Lazarus has been with the agency network
for more than three decades. After rising through
the ranks of account management and playing a
pivotal role on many of Ogilvy & Mather's signature
accounts—including American Express, Kraft, and
Unilever—she left the general agency to become
General Manager for Ogilvy & Mather Direct in the
United States.

Her success there led to positions of increasing
responsibility, from President of Ogilvy & Mather
Advertising in New York in 1991 to President of

Ogilvy North America three years later. Just one year later, she became Chief Operating Officer and President of Ogilvy & Mather Worldwide. She was named CEO in 1996 and became Chairman in 1997.

Ms. Lazarus was named Woman of the Year in 2002 by the Direct Marketing Association. She has appeared in *Fortune* magazine's annual ranking of America's 50 Most Powerful Women in Business for ten years since the list's inception in 1998. She was also the first woman to receive Columbia Business School's Distinguished Leader in Business Award.

Ms. Lazarus serves on the boards of several corporate, philanthropic, and academic institutions: General Electric, Merck, New York Presbyterian Hospital, American Museum of Natural History, Committee Encouraging Corporate Philanthropy, World Wildlife Fund, and the Board of Overseers of Columbia Business School, where she received her MBA in 1970.

Clive Mather is the former President and CEO of Shell Canada.

Clive Mather's career at Shell has spanned thirty-five years and encompassed all of its major businesses, including assignments in Brunei, Gabon, South Africa, the Netherlands, and the United Kingdom. He was appointed President and CEO of Shell Canada in August 2004, a position he held until retiring in June 2007.

About the Contributors

Prior to this position, Mr. Mather was Chairman of Shell UK and Head of Global Learning in Shell International. He also held numerous positions at the senior management level, with Group responsibility for Information Technology, Leadership Development, Contract and Procurement, eBusiness, and International Affairs.

An advocate of leadership and corporate social responsibility issues, Mr. Mather has held many public appointments in the United Kingdom, including Commissioner for the Equal Opportunities Commission and Chairman of the UK Government/Industry CSR Academy.

Mr. Mather is Chairman of the Shell Pensions Trust Ltd. and also serves on the Royal Anniversary Trust, the Council of The Garden Tomb (Jerusalem) Association, and the Advisory Board of the Relationships Foundation.

Perween Warsi is the Founder and CEO of S&A Foods, which produces Indian cuisine for the U.K. and European markets.

Ms. Warsi began her career making ethnic finger foods in her kitchen. In 1986 she founded S&A Foods, winning her first major contract to supply chilled and frozen dishes to ASDA and Safeway stores, having secured the contract via blind tasting and much perseverance.

As S&A Foods became increasingly successful, she realized that larger premises were needed to accommodate the growing business. By 1989 the first factory was built in Derby, creating over one hundred jobs for the area.

In 1996, with S&A Foods' continuing success and the need for expansion, a new factory was built next to the original site.

Ms. Warsi believes firmly in building a team of highly qualified people around her and in developing a strong "family" culture among employees.

Philip Williamson is the Former Chief Executive of Nationwide Building Society.

Mr. Williamson spent the first two decades of his career at Lloyds Bank, a company he first joined as a graduate management trainee. During his time there he spent three months at Harvard Business School.

He then spent two years with the property group UK Land before joining Nationwide in 1991 to head up the commercial lending area of the business.

In 1994 he was promoted to Divisional Director and held the roles of Marketing and Commercial Director and Retail Operations Director. He was appointed to the board in April 1996 and became Chief Executive in January 2002. Mr. Williamson retired in March 2007.

He is currently Chairman of Investors in People UK, a position he has held since 2006. He has also served as the U.K. Vice President and later President of the European Mortgage Federation.

⊰ ACKNOWLEDGMENTS ⊱

First and foremost, a heartfelt thanks goes to all of the executives who have candidly shared their hard-won experience and battle-tested insights for the *Lessons Learned* series.

Angelia Herrin at Harvard Business Publishing has consistently offered unwavering support, good humor, and counsel from the inception of this ambitious project.

Brian Surette and David Goehring provided invaluable editorial direction, perspective, and encouragement, particularly for this second series. Many thanks to the entire HBP team of designers, copy editors, and marketing professionals who helped bring this series to life.

Much appreciation goes to Jennifer Lynn and Christopher Benoît for research and diligent attention to detail, and to Roberto de Vicq de Cumptich for his imaginative cover designs.

Finally, thanks to our fellow cofounder James MacKinnon and the entire 50 Lessons team for the tremendous amount of time, effort, and steadfast support of this project.

—Adam Sodowick and Andy Hasoon
Directors and Cofounders, 50 Lessons

THE LAST PAGE IS
ONLY THE BEGINNING

Watch Free *Lessons Learned*
Video Interviews and Get Additional Resources

You've just read first-hand accounts from the business
world's top leaders, but the learning doesn't have to
end there. 50 Lessons gives you access to:

**Exclusive videos featuring the leaders
profiled in this book**

**Practical advice for putting their
insights into action**

**Challenging questions that
extend your learning**

FREE ONLINE AT:
www.50lessons.com/people